D0641126

Passages

Passages

A TREASURY

OF NEW BEGINNINGS

Illustrations by Philippe Lardy

RUNNING PRESS

PHILADELPHIA · LONDON

A Running Press Miniature Edition™
© 1997 by Running Press
Printed in China

Library of Congress Cataloging-in-Publication Number
96-71941
ISBN 0-7624-0150-8

This book may be ordered by mail from the publisher.
Please include $1.00 for postage and handling.
But try your bookstore first!

Running Press Book Publishers
125 South Twenty-second Street
Philadelphia, Pennsylvania 19103-4399

Contents

Introduction

Everything that we really accept
undergoes a change.
Katherine Mansfield

Births, deaths, graduations, retirements, new careers, new homes, new thoughts, new perspectives—human life moves in cycles filled with transition and change.

Sometimes change is abrupt and devastating; other times it is gradual, almost imperceptible.

7

Passages

Sometimes it brings us closer to long-desired goals; other times it carries us to the brink of despair. But always it is an opportunity for new growth and a passage into a life of renewed energy and deeper meaning.

With each ending comes a new beginning. The key lies in recognizing the paths and possibilities that open up to us. We must seize the opportunities presented by change, hold on to them, and shape them into goals. These actions often determine our success. It can be challenging, even frightening—but if it weren't, there would be no growth.

Within these pages, generations of writers, poets, philosophers, actors, artists, leaders, and other voices of wisdom share their thoughts on coping with transition, awakening to possibilities, keeping an open mind, and exploring new horizons. The men and women whose words appear in this collection all have traveled along different paths to arrive at the same conclusion: life is change, and embracing change empowers us to define our own destinies.

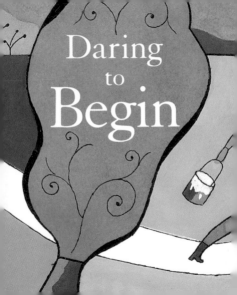

Daring
to
Begin

All glory comes from daring to begin.

Eugene F. Ware (1841–1911)
American poet

Daring to Begin

IF I SHOOT AT THE sun
I MAY HIT A star.

P. T. Barnum (1810–1891)
American showman

Passages

THE work OF AN individual

STILL REMAINS THE spark

THAT *moves*

mankind

FORWARD.

Igor Sikorsky (1889–1972)
Russian-born American engineer

HE WHO seizes

THE right moment,

IS THE right man.

J. W. von Goethe (1749–1832)
German poet

LIGHT tomorrow WITH today.

Elizabeth Barrett Browning (1806–1861)
English poet

You must
be the change
you wish to see
in the world.

Mohandas Ghandi (1869–1948)
Indian leader

There's no such word as can't.

Constance Clayton (b. 1937)
American superintendent

Daring to Begin

Determine THAT THE

THING CAN AND SHALL

be done,

AND THEN *we shall*

FIND THE WAY.

Abraham Lincoln (1809–1865)
American president

Within each of us
lies the power of our consent
to health and to sickness,
to riches and to poverty,
to freedom and to slavery.
It is we who control these,
and not another.

Richard Bach (b. 1936)
American writer

To be on the
cutting edge, you need
an edge to cut with.
That edge is your belief
in yourself
sharp and ready to go.

Sara Ryan
American artist

THOUGHTS ARE energy.

AND YOU CAN MAKE YOUR WORLD

OR BREAK YOUR WORLD

BY your thinking.

Susan L. Taylor (b. 1946)
American journalist

Daring to Begin

THERE IS something
IN EVERY one of you
THAT WAITS AND LISTENS
FOR THE sound OF THE
genuine IN YOURSELF.

Howard Thurman (b. 1900)
American cleric

27

If you're trying to do
something really well,
you're constantly questioning
yourself. Self-doubt, I think
is what it is. To renew and
reaffirm what you do, you have
to do it on a daily basis.

Yo Yo Ma (b. 1955)
Chinese-born American cellist

Daring to Begin

Asking the proper question is
the central action
of transformation. . . .
Questions are the key that cause
the secret doors of
the psyche to swing open.

Clarissa Pinkola Estés (b. 1943)
American writer and psychologist

Passages

NOTHING CONTRIBUTES SO MUCH

TO tranquilize the mind

AS A steady purpose—

A POINT ON WHICH *the soul*

MAY FIX ITS

INTELLECTUAL EYE.

Mary Shelley (1797–1851)
English writer

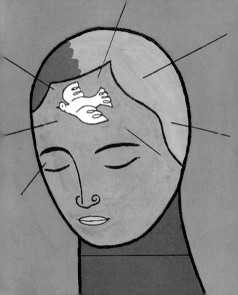

Patience AND passage of time DO MORE THAN strength AND fury.

Jean de La Fontaine (1621–1695)
French poet

Never give up.
KEEP YOUR thoughts AND
YOUR mind ALWAYS
ON THE goal.

Tom Bradley (1917–1998)
American politician

The greatest
achievements
were at first and
for sometime
dreams.

James Allen (1864–1912)
English writer

Dreams are
the soul's pantry.
Keep it
well stocked and
your soul will
never hunger.

Cindy Williams (b. 1947)
American actress

THERE IS NOTHING like a dream
TO create THE future.
Utopia TODAY,
flesh and blood
TOMORROW.

Victor Hugo (1802–1885)
French writer

IT'S THE possibility OF
HAVING A DREAM come true
THAT MAKES life INTERESTING . . .

Paulo Coelho
Latin American writer

... care TO HAVE A DREAM.

BE SURE TO HAVE a dream.

Dinah Shore (1920–1994)
American entertainer

41

A MAN WILL SOMETIMES devote ALL his life TO THE DEVELOPMENT OF ONE PART OF HIS BODY—THE wishbone.

Robert Frost (1874–1963)
American poet

Daring to Begin

IF OUTRAGEOUS imagination IS THE WINE OF madness, THEN COME fill my cup.

Sheldon Kopp (b. 1929)
American psychologist and writer

43

Passages

Hope IS THE

source OF strength.

WE CAN DEPEND ON

OUR arms AND hands,

BUT WE CAN'T DO *anything*

WITHOUT HOPE.

Starkhawk [Miriam Simos] (b. 1915)
American writer and activist

. . . if one advances confidently
in the direction of his dreams,
and endeavors to live the life
which he has imagined,
he will meet with a success
unexpected in common hours.

Henry David Thoreau (1817–1862)
American writer

Daring to Begin

Most people seem to
be interested in turning their
dreams into reality.
Then there are those who turn
reality into dreams.
I belong to the latter group.

Allen Say (b. 1937)
Chinese-born American writer

It is time NOW FOR US TO RISE from sleep.

Saint Benedict (480–547)
Italian missionary

THE world IS BEFORE YOU,

AND YOU NEED NOT take it

OR leave it

AS IT WAS WHEN YOU CAME IN.

James Baldwin (1924–1987)
American writer

Striving
for
Growth

. . . we have to grow,
we have to
move forward,
to learn and evolve,
add to our
dictionary of life.

Janet Leigh
American actress

Striving for Growth

Nothing is lost upon a man who
is bent upon growth; nothing
wasted on one who is always
preparing for . . . life by keeping
eyes, mind and heart open
to nature, men, books, experience
. . . and what he gathers serves
him at unexpected moments
in unforeseen ways.

Hamilton Wright Mabie (1845–1916)
American editor and critic

53

True life IS LIVED WHEN
tiny changes OCCUR.

Leo Tolstoy (1828–1910)
Russian writer

Striving for Growth

DAY AFTER DAY, WE discover

OUR OWN LIVES. BECAUSE WE NEVER

KNOW WHAT WE will find,

EVERY DISCOVERY IS

AN unexpected gift

WE GIVE TO OURSELVES.

Barbara J. Esbensen
American poet

We make progress by
a constant spiraling back
and forth between the
inner world and the
outer one, the personal
and the political, the self
and the circumstances.
Nature doesn't move
in a straight line, and
as part of nature,
neither do we.

Gloria Steinem (b. 1934)
American activist, writer, and editor

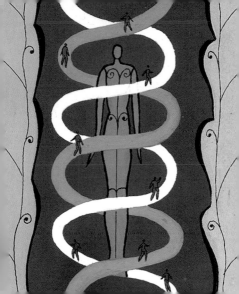

Like the proverbial pebble
dropped into a still pond,
the shifts of consciousness
we make in our personal lives
send out tiny but important
waves that ripple over the
surface of the whole.

Shakti Gawain (b. 1948)
American writer

Everything
that we really
accept
undergoes a
change.

Katherine Mansfield (1888–1923)
American writer

Striving for Growth

It's not difficult to coast along when things are *going well*, when a balance has been established. What's difficult is the new. The new ice. The new light, the new feelings.

Peter Hoag (b. 1957)
Danish writer

Some steps must be taken
defiantly, against the grain.
There is no growth without
a bursting, without pain:
primitive peoples in their
wisdom place pain
at the center of initiation.

John Updike (b. 1932)
American writer

62

If there is no struggle, there is no progress.

Frederick Douglass (1817–1895)
American abolitionist

Passages

IF WE HAD NO winter,
THE spring WOULD NOT BE SO PLEASANT:
IF WE DID NOT SOMETIMES
TASTE OF adversity,
prosperity WOULD
NOT BE SO WELCOME.

Anne Bradstreet (1612–1672)
American poet

ALTHOUGH the world IS VERY FULL OF SUFFERING,

IT IS ALSO FULL OF THE

overcoming OF IT.

Helen Keller (1880–1968)
American writer and lecturer

What the
caterpillar calls
the end
of the world,
the master calls
a butterfly.

Richard Bach (b. 1936)
American writer

All changes,
even the most longed for,
have their melancholy;
for what we leave behind us is
a part of ourselves;
we must die to one life before
we can enter another.

Anatole France (1844–1924)
French writer

Striving for Growth

FIND EXPRESSION FOR SORROW,

AND IT WILL BECOME dear to you.

FIND EXPRESSION FOR A joy,

AND IT

WILL *intensify*

ITS ECSTASY.

Oscar Wilde (1854–1900)
Irish poet and playwright

71

Passages

. . . TO look back IS

A TASK. IT IS LIKE RE-ENTERING

A trap, OR A LABYRINTH,

FROM WHICH ONE HAS ONLY TOO LATELY,

AND TOO NARROWLY, escaped.

Louise Bogan (1897–1970)
American poet and critic

Striving for Growth

I ONLY know THERE

CAME TO ME. . . .

A sense OF

GLAD awakening.

Edna Saint Vincent Millay (1892–1950)
American poet

Passages

BUT THERE ISN'T ANY SECOND
HALF OF myself WAITING
TO plug in AND
MAKE ME WHOLE. IT'S THERE.
I'm already whole.

Sally Field (b. 1947)
American actress

Striving for Growth

As we slowly awaken,

we notice the maturing of certain

qualities of mind.

Stephen Levine
American writer

Great results
cannot be achieved
at once, and we
must be satisfied to
advance in life as
we walk—
step by step.

Samuel Smiles (1812–1904)
Scottish biographer

My way is to begin with the beginning.

George Gordon, Lord Byron (1788–1824)
English poet

The beginning is always today.

Mary Wollstonecraft
American women's rights advocate

Run a moist pen slick through everything and start afresh.

Charles Dickens (1812–1870)
English writer

Tomorrow is the
most important thing in life.
Comes into us
at midnight very clean.
It's perfect when it arrives and
puts itself in our hands.
It hopes we've learned
something from yesterday.

John Wayne (b. 1906)
American actor

Grab A chance
AND YOU WON'T be sorry
FOR A
might
HAVE BEEN.

Arthur Ransome (1884–1967)
English writer

To live IS TO THINK AND ACT,
AND TO think AND act
IS TO change.

James Allen (1864–1912)
English writer

SOMEDAY change WILL BE
ACCEPTED as life ITSELF.

Shirley Maclaine (b. 1934)
American actress and writer

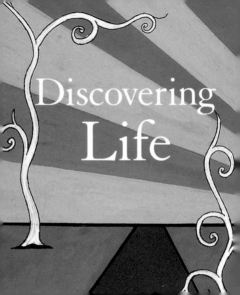

Discovering
Life

To every man

HIS OWN life

is A

MYSTERY.

Latin proverb

Life WAS MEANT TO BE A mystery. TO BE lived SPONTANEOUSLY FROM A present time, UNPREDICTABLE place.

Judy Wardell
American writer

Discovering Life

LIFE IS easier THAN YOU'D THINK;

ALL THAT IS NECESSARY

IS TO accept THE IMPOSSIBLE,

do WITHOUT THE INDISPENSABLE,

AND bear THE INTOLERABLE.

Kathleen Norris (1880–1966)
American novelist

You must learn
day by day, year by year,
to broaden your horizon.
The more things you love,
the more you are interested in,
the more you enjoy,
the more you are indignant
about—the more you have left
when anything happens.

Ethel Barrymore (1879–1959)
American actress

All life
is an experiment.

Oliver Wendell Holmes Jr. (1841–1935)
American jurist

No sooner do
we think we have
assembled a
comfortable life
than we find a piece
of ourselves
that has
no place to fit in.

Gail Sheehy (b. 1937)
American writer and social critic

Life IS NOT

A MATTER OF HOLDING GOOD CARDS,

BUT OF playing

A *poor hand*

WELL.

Robert Louis Stevenson (1850–1894)
Scottish writer

SHE HAD NOTHING

AGAINST developing . . .

DEVELOPMENT, CHANGE, RIPENING,

were life.

Mary A. Arnim (1866–1941)
English writer

Discovering Life

ALL CHANGE IS a miracle

TO CONTEMPLATE; BUT IT IS

A MIRACLE WHICH IS TAKING PLACE

every instant.

Henry David Thoreau (1817–1862)
American writer

No trumpets
sound when the
important decisions
of our life are made.
Destiny is made
known silently.

Agnes De Mille (1905–1993)
American dancer

We are well advised
to keep on nodding terms with
the people we used to be,
whether we find them attractive
company or not. . . .
We forget all too soon
the things we thought we could
never forget.

Joan Didion (b. 1934)
American writer

Life IS accepting WHAT IS AND working FROM THAT.

Gloria Naylor (b. 1950)
American writer

Discovering Life

THIS earthly world IS

OUR WORK ROOM, OUR LABORATORY.

THIS IS WHERE WE

figure out HOW TO DO IT.

Barbara Callahan
American writer and editor

THE GREAT AND GLORIOUS

masterpiece OF MAN

IS HOW

TO *live*

WITH PURPOSE.

Michel de Montaigne (1533–1592)
French writer

Passages

I WISH TO LIVE
BECAUSE life HAS WITH IT
THAT WHICH IS good,
THAT WHICH IS beautiful,
AND THAT WHICH IS love.

Lorraine Hansberry (1930–1965)
American playwright

AND ANOTHER truth.

THAT THERE ARE NO SECRET

PASSAGES TO strength,

NO magic words.

IT IS JUST SOMETHING

YOU KNOW ABOUT yourself.

Judith Guest
American writer

A man is
happy so long
as he chooses
to be happy and
nothing can
stop him.

Alexander Solzhenitsyn (b. 1918)
Russian writer

You conquer fate by thought.

Henry David Thoreau (1817–1862)
American writer

Sometimes people
will say something you don't
like . . . You let it go by, even if
you really would like to choke
'em. By smiling, I think I've
made more friends than if I was
the other way.

Ella Fitzgerald (1917–1996)
American singer

Life has its pain and evil . . .
but like a good novel . . .
there is infinite joy in seeing
the World, the most interesting
of continued stories, unfold,
even though one misses the end.

W. E. B. Du Bois (1868–1963)
American writer

Nothing can bring you peace but yourself.

Ralph Waldo Emerson (1803–1882)
American writer

Discovering Life

Life IS MADE UP OF desires THAT
SEEM big AND vital ONE MINUTE,
AND little AND absurd THE NEXT.

I GUESS WE GET

WHAT'S *best* FOR US

IN THE END.

Alice Caldwell Rose
American writer

Passages

WE ARE rich ONLY THROUGH

WHAT we give,

AND poor ONLY THROUGH

WHAT we refuse.

Anne-Sophie Swetchine (1782–1857)
Russian-born French writer

THREE THINGS IN HUMAN life ARE IMPORTANT.

THE first IS TO BE KIND.

THE second IS TO BE KIND.

AND THE third IS TO BE KIND.

Henry James (1811–1882)
American writer

Passages

SOMETIMES WHEN I CONSIDER

WHAT TREMENDOUS consequences

COME FROM little things,

A CHANCE WORD, A TAP ON THE SHOULDER,

. . . I AM *tempted to think* . . .

THERE ARE NO LITTLE THINGS.

Bruce Barton (1886–1967)
American executive and writer

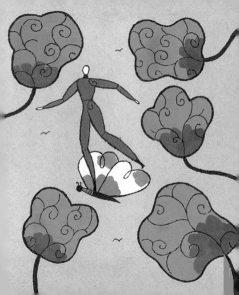

We must hold
in our minds these utterly
contradictory thoughts:
not one of us matters at all;
each of us is
infinitely precious.

Jane Emily Bowers
American botanist

What we call the
beginning is often the end.
And to make an
end is to make a beginning.
The end is
where we start from.

T. S. Eliot (1888–1965)
American-born British poet

This book has been bound
using handcraft methods, and was Smyth-sewn
to ensure durability.

The cover and interior were illustrated
by Philippe Lardy.

The cover and interior were designed
by Maria Taffera Lewis.

The text was edited by Gena M. Pearson.

The text was set in Granjon and
Helvetica Neue Condensed.